Dear Creator,

Consumer reviews are one of the most powerful tools to build your audience and gain trust with your viewers and followers. Not only that, but it's extremely helpful to other consumers looking a potential purchase.

There's a reason why brands pay influencers to review products; it's because they know that word of mouth through the proven system really works!
Reviewing products is great way to grow your business carefully and honestly for youtube, instagram, tiktok or blog.

Use this "Makeup Journal" to keep track of reviews, ratings, and thoughts while on the go. 31 days of plenty of space for jotting down reviews and keeping track of your honest thoughts on the products you use.

This Makeup Journal Belongs To:,

_____

# 31

# DAY MAKEUP
# REVIEW LOG

## JOURNALING FOR SUCCESS

## MNY

Printed by MNY Publications

First printing, 2022.

Mine, Now Yours Publications
P.O. Box 32471
Bellingham, WA, 98228

www.minenowyourspublications.com

"The most beautiful makeup on a woman is passion, but cosmetics are easier to buy."

Yves Saint Laurent.

-

# My Makeup Reviews

Product Name?

_____

_____

_____

Product Use?

_____

_____

_____

How was it applied?

_____

_____

_____

Was it easy to work with?

_____

_____

_____

# Likes & Performance

## What did you like/dislike?
_____
_____
_____

## How did it last/wear/feel?
_____
_____
_____

## How did it perform?
_____
_____
_____

## Worth the purchase or waste of money?
_____
_____
_____

# Ratings & Thoughts

Were there any deal-breakers?

_____

_____

_____

Did you try it with other products? (e.g. primer, setting powder, etc.)

_____

_____

Bubble in how many stars does this product gets!

☆☆☆☆☆

Final Review...

_____

_____

_____

_____

# My Makeup Reviews

Product Name?

Product Use?

How was it applied?

Was it easy to work with?

# Likes & Performance

What did you like/dislike?

_____

_____

_____

How did it last/wear/feel?

_____

_____

_____

How did it perform?

_____

_____

_____

Worth the purchase or waste of money?

_____

_____

_____

# Ratings & Thoughts

Were there any deal-breakers?

_____

_____

_____

Did you try it with other products? (e.g. primer, setting powder, etc.)

_____

_____

Bubble in how many stars does this product gets!

☆☆☆☆☆

Final Review...

_____

_____

_____

_____

# My Makeup Reviews

Product Name?

_____

_____

_____

Product Use?

_____

_____

_____

How was it applied?

_____

_____

_____

Was it easy to work with?

_____

_____

_____

# Likes & Performance

## What did you like/dislike?

## How did it last/wear/feel?

## How did it perform?

## Worth the purchase or waste of money?

# Ratings & Thoughts

Were there any deal-breakers?

_____

_____

_____

Did you try it with other products? (e.g. primer, setting powder, etc.)

_____

_____

Bubble in how many stars does this product gets!

☆☆☆☆☆

Final Review...

_____

_____

_____

_____

# My Makeup Reviews

Product Name?

_____

_____

_____

Product Use?

_____

_____

_____

How was it applied?

_____

_____

_____

Was it easy to work with?

_____

_____

_____

# Likes & Performance

What did you like/dislike?

_____

_____

_____

How did it last/wear/feel?

_____

_____

_____

How did it perform?

_____

_____

_____

Worth the purchase or waste of money?

_____

_____

_____

# Ratings & Thoughts

Were there any deal-breakers?

_____

_____

_____

Did you try it with other products? (e.g. primer, setting powder, etc.)

_____

_____

Bubble in how many stars does this product gets!

☆☆☆☆☆

Final Review...

_____

_____

_____

_____

# My Makeup Reviews

Product Name?

_____

_____

_____

Product Use?

_____

_____

_____

How was it applied?

_____

_____

_____

Was it easy to work with?

_____

_____

_____

# Likes & Performance

## What did you like/dislike?

_____
_____
_____
_____

## How did it last/wear/feel?

_____
_____
_____
_____

## How did it perform?

_____
_____
_____
_____

## Worth the purchase or waste of money?

_____
_____
_____
_____

# Ratings & Thoughts

Were there any deal-breakers?

_____

_____

_____

Did you try it with other products? (e.g. primer, setting powder, etc.)

_____

_____

Bubble in how many stars does this product gets!

☆☆☆☆☆

Final Review...

_____

_____

_____

_____

# My Makeup Reviews

**Product Name?**

_____

_____

_____

**Product Use?**

_____

_____

_____

**How was it applied?**

_____

_____

_____

**Was it easy to work with?**

_____

_____

_____

# Likes & Performance

What did you like/dislike?

_____

_____

_____

How did it last/wear/feel?

_____

_____

_____

How did it perform?

_____

_____

_____

Worth the purchase or waste of money?

_____

_____

_____

# Ratings & Thoughts

Were there any deal-breakers?

_____

_____

_____

Did you try it with other products? (e.g. primer, setting powder, etc.)

_____

_____

Bubble in how many stars does this product gets!

☆☆☆☆☆

Final Review...

_____

_____

_____

_____

*My Makeup Reviews*

Product Name?
_____
_____
_____

Product Use?
_____
_____
_____

How was it applied?
_____
_____
_____

Was it easy to work with?
_____
_____
_____

*Likes & Performance*

## What did you like/dislike?

_____

_____

_____

## How did it last/wear/feel?

_____

_____

_____

## How did it perform?

_____

_____

_____

## Worth the purchase or waste of money?

_____

_____

_____

# Ratings & Thoughts

Were there any deal-breakers?

_____

_____

_____

Did you try it with other products? (e.g. primer, setting powder, etc.)

_____

_____

Bubble in how many stars does this product gets!

☆ ☆ ☆ ☆ ☆

Final Review...

_____

_____

_____

_____

# My Makeup Reviews

Product Name?

_____

_____

_____

Product Use?

_____

_____

_____

How was it applied?

_____

_____

_____

Was it easy to work with?

_____

_____

_____

# Likes & Performance

## What did you like/dislike?

_____

_____

_____

## How did it last/wear/feel?

_____

_____

_____

## How did it perform?

_____

_____

_____

## Worth the purchase or waste of money?

_____

_____

_____

# Ratings & Thoughts

Were there any deal-breakers?

_____

_____

_____

Did you try it with other products? (e.g. primer, setting powder, etc.)

_____

_____

Bubble in how many stars does this product gets!

☆☆☆☆☆

Final Review...

_____

_____

_____

_____

# My Makeup Reviews

## Product Name?

---

---

---

## Product Use?

---

---

---

## How was it applied?

---

---

---

## Was it easy to work with?

---

---

---

*Likes & Performance*

What did you like/dislike?

_____

_____

_____

How did it last/wear/feel?

_____

_____

_____

How did it perform?

_____

_____

_____

Worth the purchase or waste of money?

_____

_____

_____

# Ratings & Thoughts

Were there any deal-breakers?

_____

_____

_____

Did you try it with other products? (e.g. primer, setting powder, etc.)

_____

_____

Bubble in how many stars does this product gets!

☆☆☆☆☆

Final Review...

_____

_____

_____

_____

# My Makeup Reviews

### Product Name?

### Product Use?

### How was it applied?

### Was it easy to work with?

# Likes & Performance

What did you like/dislike?

_____

_____

_____

How did it last/wear/feel?

_____

_____

_____

How did it perform?

_____

_____

_____

Worth the purchase or waste of money?

_____

_____

_____

# *Ratings & Thoughts*

Were there any deal-breakers?

Did you try it with other products? (e.g. primer, setting powder, etc.)

Bubble in how many stars does this product gets!

☆☆☆☆☆

Final Review...

# My Makeup Reviews

Product Name?

_____

_____

_____

Product Use?

_____

_____

_____

How was it applied?

_____

_____

_____

Was it easy to work with?

_____

_____

_____

# Likes & Performance

What did you like/dislike?

_____

_____

_____

_____

How did it last/wear/feel?

_____

_____

_____

_____

How did it perform?

_____

_____

_____

_____

Worth the purchase or waste of money?

_____

_____

_____

_____

# Ratings & Thoughts

Were there any deal-breakers?

_____

_____

_____

Did you try it with other products? (e.g.
primer, setting powder, etc.)

_____

_____

Bubble in how many stars does this
product gets!

☆☆☆☆☆

Final Review...

_____

_____

_____

_____

# My Makeup Reviews

Product Name?

_____

_____

_____

Product Use?

_____

_____

_____

How was it applied?

_____

_____

_____

Was it easy to work with?

_____

_____

_____

# Likes & Performance

What did you like/dislike?

_____

_____

_____

How did it last/wear/feel?

_____

_____

_____

How did it perform?

_____

_____

_____

Worth the purchase or waste of money?

_____

_____

_____

# Ratings & Thoughts

Were there any deal-breakers?

_____

_____

_____

Did you try it with other products? (e.g. primer, setting powder, etc.)

_____

_____

Bubble in how many stars does this product gets!

☆☆☆☆☆

Final Review...

_____

_____

_____

_____

# My Makeup Reviews

**Product Name?**

_____

_____

_____

**Product Use?**

_____

_____

_____

**How was it applied?**

_____

_____

_____

**Was it easy to work with?**

_____

_____

_____

# Likes & Performance

## What did you like/dislike?

_____

_____

_____

## How did it last/wear/feel?

_____

_____

_____

## How did it perform?

_____

_____

_____

## Worth the purchase or waste of money?

_____

_____

_____

## Ratings & Thoughts

Were there any deal-breakers?

_____

_____

_____

Did you try it with other products? (e.g. primer, setting powder, etc.)

_____

_____

Bubble in how many stars does this product gets!

☆☆☆☆☆

Final Review...

_____

_____

_____

_____

# My Makeup Reviews

Product Name?

_____

_____

_____

Product Use?

_____

_____

_____

How was it applied?

_____

_____

_____

Was it easy to work with?

_____

_____

_____

# Likes & Performance

What did you like/dislike?
_____
_____
_____

How did it last/wear/feel?
_____
_____
_____

How did it perform?
_____
_____
_____

Worth the purchase or waste of money?
_____
_____
_____

# Ratings & Thoughts

Were there any deal-breakers?

_____

_____

_____

Did you try it with other products? (e.g.
primer, setting powder, etc.)

_____

_____

Bubble in how many stars does this
product gets!

☆☆☆☆☆

Final Review...

_____

_____

_____

_____

# My Makeup Reviews

**Product Name?**

---
---
---

**Product Use?**

---
---
---

**How was it applied?**

---
---
---

**Was it easy to work with?**

---
---
---

# Likes & Performance

What did you like/dislike?

_____

_____

_____

How did it last/wear/feel?

_____

_____

_____

How did it perform?

_____

_____

_____

Worth the purchase or waste of money?

_____

_____

_____

Were there any deal-breakers?

_____

_____

_____

Did you try it with other products? (e.g.
primer, setting powder, etc.)

_____

_____

Bubble in how many stars does this
product gets!

☆ ☆ ☆ ☆ ☆

Final Review...

_____

_____

_____

_____

# My Makeup Reviews

### Product Name?

_____

_____

_____

### Product Use?

_____

_____

_____

### How was it applied?

_____

_____

_____

### Was it easy to work with?

_____

_____

_____

*Likes & Performance*

What did you like/dislike?

_____

_____

_____

How did it last/wear/feel?

_____

_____

_____

How did it perform?

_____

_____

_____

Worth the purchase or waste of money?

_____

_____

_____

# Ratings & Thoughts

Were there any deal-breakers?

_____

_____

_____

Did you try it with other products? (e.g. primer, setting powder, etc.)

_____

_____

Bubble in how many stars does this product gets!

☆☆☆☆☆

Final Review...

_____

_____

_____

_____

# My Makeup Reviews

### Product Name?

_____

_____

_____

### Product Use?

_____

_____

_____

### How was it applied?

_____

_____

_____

### Was it easy to work with?

_____

_____

_____

# Likes & Performance

### What did you like/dislike?

### How did it last/wear/feel?

### How did it perform?

### Worth the purchase or waste of money?

# Ratings & Thoughts

Were there any deal-breakers?

_____

_____

_____

Did you try it with other products? (e.g. primer, setting powder, etc.)

_____

_____

Bubble in how many stars does this product gets!

☆☆☆☆☆

Final Review...

_____

_____

_____

_____

# My Makeup Reviews

## Product Name?

_____

_____

_____

## Product Use?

_____

_____

_____

## How was it applied?

_____

_____

_____

## Was it easy to work with?

_____

_____

_____

# Likes & Performance

What did you like/dislike?

_____

_____

_____

How did it last/wear/feel?

_____

_____

_____

How did it perform?

_____

_____

_____

Worth the purchase or waste of money?

_____

_____

_____

# Ratings & Thoughts

Were there any deal-breakers?

_____

_____

_____

Did you try it with other products? (e.g. primer, setting powder, etc.)

_____

_____

Bubble in how many stars does this product gets!

☆☆☆☆☆

Final Review...

_____

_____

_____

_____

My Makeup Reviews

Product Name?

_____

_____

_____

Product Use?

_____

_____

_____

How was it applied?

_____

_____

_____

Was it easy to work with?

_____

_____

_____

# Likes & Performance

## What did you like/dislike?

_____
_____
_____

## How did it last/wear/feel?

_____
_____
_____

## How did it perform?

_____
_____
_____

## Worth the purchase or waste of money?

_____
_____
_____

# Ratings & Thoughts

Were there any deal-breakers?

_____

_____

_____

Did you try it with other products? (e.g. primer, setting powder, etc.)

_____

_____

Bubble in how many stars does this product gets!

☆☆☆☆☆

Final Review...

_____

_____

_____

_____

# My Makeup Reviews

### Product Name?

_____

_____

_____

### Product Use?

_____

_____

_____

### How was it applied?

_____

_____

_____

### Was it easy to work with?

_____

_____

_____

# Likes & Performance

What did you like/dislike?

How did it last/wear/feel?

How did it perform?

Worth the purchase or waste of money?

# Ratings & Thoughts

Were there any deal-breakers?

_____

_____

_____

Did you try it with other products? (e.g. primer, setting powder, etc.)

_____

_____

Bubble in how many stars does this product gets!

☆ ☆ ☆ ☆ ☆

Final Review...

_____

_____

_____

_____

# My Makeup Reviews

**Product Name?**

_____

_____

_____

**Product Use?**

_____

_____

_____

**How was it applied?**

_____

_____

_____

**Was it easy to work with?**

_____

_____

_____

# Likes & Performance

What did you like/dislike?

How did it last/wear/feel?

How did it perform?

Worth the purchase or waste of money?

# Ratings & Thoughts

## Were there any deal-breakers?

_____

_____

_____

## Did you try it with other products? (e.g. primer, setting powder, etc.)

_____

_____

## Bubble in how many stars does this product gets!

☆ ☆ ☆ ☆ ☆

## Final Review...

_____

_____

_____

_____

# My Makeup Reviews

Product Name?

_____

_____

_____

Product Use?

_____

_____

_____

How was it applied?

_____

_____

_____

Was it easy to work with?

_____

_____

_____

# Likes & Performance

What did you like/dislike?

_____

_____

_____

How did it last/wear/feel?

_____

_____

_____

How did it perform?

_____

_____

_____

Worth the purchase or waste of money?

_____

_____

_____

# Ratings & Thoughts

Were there any deal-breakers?

_____

_____

_____

Did you try it with other products? (e.g. primer, setting powder, etc.)

_____

_____

Bubble in how many stars does this product gets!

☆☆☆☆☆

Final Review...

_____

_____

_____

_____

# My Makeup Reviews

Product Name?

_____

_____

_____

Product Use?

_____

_____

_____

How was it applied?

_____

_____

_____

Was it easy to work with?

_____

_____

_____

# Likes & Performance

What did you like/dislike?

_____

_____

_____

How did it last/wear/feel?

_____

_____

_____

How did it perform?

_____

_____

_____

Worth the purchase or waste of money?

_____

_____

_____

# Ratings & Thoughts

**Were there any deal-breakers?**

_____
_____
_____

**Did you try it with other products? (e.g. primer, setting powder, etc.)**

_____
_____
_____

**Bubble in how many stars does this product gets!**

☆☆☆☆☆

**Final Review...**

_____
_____
_____
_____

# My Makeup Reviews

Product Name?

_____

_____

_____

Product Use?

_____

_____

_____

How was it applied?

_____

_____

_____

Was it easy to work with?

_____

_____

_____

# Likes & Performance

What did you like/dislike?

How did it last/wear/feel?

How did it perform?

Worth the purchase or waste of money?

# Ratings & Thoughts

Were there any deal-breakers?

_____

_____

_____

Did you try it with other products? (e.g. primer, setting powder, etc.)

_____

_____

Bubble in how many stars does this product gets!

☆☆☆☆☆

Final Review...

_____

_____

_____

_____

# My Makeup Reviews

**Product Name?**

_____

_____

_____

**Product Use?**

_____

_____

_____

**How was it applied?**

_____

_____

_____

**Was it easy to work with?**

_____

_____

_____

# Likes & Performance

What did you like/dislike?

How did it last/wear/feel?

How did it perform?

Worth the purchase or waste of money?

# Ratings & Thoughts

Were there any deal-breakers?

_____

_____

_____

Did you try it with other products? (e.g. primer, setting powder, etc.)

_____

_____

Bubble in how many stars does this product gets!

☆☆☆☆☆

Final Review...

_____

_____

_____

_____

*My Makeup Reviews*

Product Name?

_____
_____
_____
_____

Product Use?

_____
_____
_____

How was it applied?

_____
_____
_____

Was it easy to work with?

_____
_____
_____

# Likes & Performance

What did you like/dislike?

How did it last/wear/feel?

How did it perform?

Worth the purchase or waste of money?

# Ratings & Thoughts

Were there any deal-breakers?

_____

_____

_____

Did you try it with other products? (e.g. primer, setting powder, etc.)

_____

_____

Bubble in how many stars does this product gets!

☆☆☆☆☆

Final Review...

_____

_____

_____

_____

# My Makeup Reviews

Product Name?

Product Use?

How was it applied?

Was it easy to work with?

# Likes & Performance

## What did you like/dislike?

_____

_____

_____

## How did it last/wear/feel?

_____

_____

_____

## How did it perform?

_____

_____

_____

## Worth the purchase or waste of money?

_____

_____

_____

# Ratings & Thoughts

Were there any deal-breakers?

_____

_____

_____

Did you try it with other products? (e.g. primer, setting powder, etc.)

_____

_____

Bubble in how many stars does this product gets!

☆☆☆☆☆

Final Review...

_____

_____

_____

_____

# My Makeup Reviews

Product Name?

Product Use?

How was it applied?

Was it easy to work with?

*Likes & Performance*

What did you like/dislike?
_____
_____
_____

How did it last/wear/feel?
_____
_____
_____

How did it perform?
_____
_____
_____

Worth the purchase or waste of money?
_____
_____
_____

# Ratings & Thoughts

Were there any deal-breakers?

_____

_____

_____

Did you try it with other products? (e.g. primer, setting powder, etc.)

_____

_____

Bubble in how many stars does this product gets!

☆☆☆☆☆

Final Review...

_____

_____

_____

_____

# My Makeup Reviews

### Product Name?

_____

_____

_____

### Product Use?

_____

_____

_____

### How was it applied?

_____

_____

_____

### Was it easy to work with?

_____

_____

_____

# Likes & Performance

## What did you like/dislike?

_____

_____

_____

_____

## How did it last/wear/feel?

_____

_____

_____

_____

## How did it perform?

_____

_____

_____

_____

## Worth the purchase or waste of money?

_____

_____

_____

# Ratings & Thoughts

Were there any deal-breakers?

_____

_____

_____

Did you try it with other products? (e.g. primer, setting powder, etc.)

_____

_____

Bubble in how many stars does this product gets!

☆☆☆☆☆

Final Review...

_____

_____

_____

_____

# My Makeup Reviews

**Product Name?**

_____

_____

_____

**Product Use?**

_____

_____

_____

**How was it applied?**

_____

_____

_____

**Was it easy to work with?**

_____

_____

_____

# Likes & Performance

What did you like/dislike?

_____

_____

_____

How did it last/wear/feel?

_____

_____

_____

How did it perform?

_____

_____

_____

Worth the purchase or waste of money?

_____

_____

_____

# Ratings & Thoughts

Were there any deal-breakers?

_____

_____

Did you try it with other products? (e.g. primer, setting powder, etc.)

_____

_____

Bubble in how many stars does this product gets!

☆☆☆☆☆

Final Review...

_____

_____

_____

_____

# My Makeup Reviews

**Product Name?**

_____

_____

_____

**Product Use?**

_____

_____

_____

**How was it applied?**

_____

_____

_____

**Was it easy to work with?**

_____

_____

_____

# Likes & Performance

What did you like/dislike?

How did it last/wear/feel?

How did it perform?

Worth the purchase or waste of money?

# *Ratings & Thoughts*

Were there any deal-breakers?

_____

_____

_____

Did you try it with other products? (e.g. primer, setting powder, etc.)

_____

_____

Bubble in how many stars does this product gets!

☆☆☆☆☆

Final Review...

_____

_____

_____

_____

# My Makeup Reviews

Product Name?

_____

_____

_____

Product Use?

_____

_____

_____

How was it applied?

_____

_____

_____

Was it easy to work with?

_____

_____

_____

# Likes & Performance

What did you like/dislike?

_____

_____

_____

How did it last/wear/feel?

_____

_____

_____

How did it perform?

_____

_____

_____

Worth the purchase or waste of money?

_____

_____

_____

# Ratings & Thoughts

Were there any deal-breakers?

_____

_____

_____

Did you try it with other products? (e.g. primer, setting powder, etc.)

_____

_____

Bubble in how many stars does this product gets!

☆☆☆☆☆

Final Review...

_____

_____

_____

_____

# Notes & Favorite Products

Made in the USA
Columbia, SC
16 November 2024

46663291R00057